ISBN 978-1-331-32052-4
PIBN 10173896

This book is a reproduction of an important historical work. Forgotten Books uses
state-of-the-art technology to digitally reconstruct the work, preserving the original format
whilst repairing imperfections present in the aged copy. In rare cases, an imperfection in
the original, such as a blemish or missing page, may be replicated in our edition. We do,
however, repair the vast majority of imperfections successfully; any imperfections that
remain are intentionally left to preserve the state of such historical works.

1 MONTH OF
FREE
READING

at

www.ForgottenBooks.com

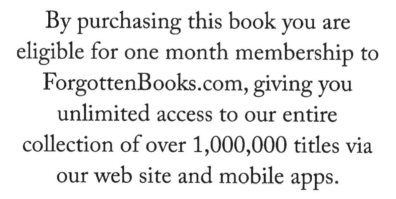

By purchasing this book you are eligible for one month membership to ForgottenBooks.com, giving you unlimited access to our entire collection of over 1,000,000 titles via our web site and mobile apps.

To claim your free month visit:

www.forgottenbooks.com/free173896

English
Français
Deutsche
Italiano
Español
Português

www.forgottenbooks.com

Mythology Photography **Fiction**
Fishing Christianity **Art** Cooking
Essays Buddhism Freemasonry
Medicine **Biology** Music **Ancient**
Egypt Evolution Carpentry Physics
Dance Geology **Mathematics** Fitness
Shakespeare **Folklore** Yoga Marketing
Confidence Immortality Biographies
Poetry **Psychology** Witchcraft
Electronics Chemistry History **Law**
Accounting **Philosophy** Anthropology
Alchemy Drama Quantum Mechanics
Atheism Sexual Health **Ancient History**
Entrepreneurship Languages Sport
Paleontology Needlework Islam
Metaphysics Investment Archaeology
Parenting Statistics Criminology
Motivational

THE FROZEN GRAIL
and Other Poems

By

ELSA BARKER

THE FROZEN GRAIL

AND OTHER POEMS

THE FROZEN GRAIL

AND OTHER POEMS

BY

ELSA BARKER

AUTHOR OF "THE SON OF MARY BETHEL"

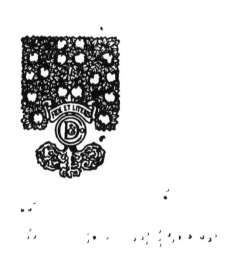

NEW YORK

DUFFIELD & COMPANY

1910

THE TROW PRESS, NEW YORK

CONTENTS

3

4

THE FROZEN GRAIL

AND OTHER POEMS

THE FROZEN GRAIL

(To Peary and his men, before the last expedition.)

WHY sing the legends of the Holy Grail,
    The dead crusaders of the Sepulchre,
While these men live? Are the great bards all dumb?
Here is a vision to shake the blood of Song,
And make Fame's watchman tremble at his post.

What shall prevail against the spirit of man,
When cold, the lean and snarling wolf of hunger,
The threatening spear of ice-mailed Solitude,
Silence, and space, and ghostly-footed Fear
Prevail not? Dante, in his frozen hell
Shivering, endured no bleakness like the void
These men have warmed with their own flaming will,
And peopled with their dreams. The wind from fierce
Arcturus in their faces, at their backs
The whip of the world's doubt, and in their souls
Courage to die—if death shall be the price
Of that cold cup that will assuage their thirst,
They climb, and fall, and stagger toward the goal.
They lay themselves the road whereby they travel,
And sue God for a franchise. Does He watch
Behind the lattice of the boreal lights?
In that grail-chapel of their stern-vowed quest,

5

Ninety of God's long paces toward the North,
Will they behold the splendour of His face?

To conquer the world must man renounce the world?
These have renounced it. Had ye only faith
Ye might move mountains, said the Nazarene.
Why, these have faith to move the zones of man
Out to the point where All and Nothing meet.
They catch the bit of Death between their teeth,
In one wild dash to trample the unknown
And leap the gates of knowledge. They have dared
Even to defy the sentinel that guards
The doors of the forbidden—dared to hurl
Their breathing bodies after the Ideal,
That like the heavenly kingdom must be taken
Only by violence. The star that leads
The leader of this quest has held the world
True to its orbit for a million years.

And shall he fail? They never fail who light
Their lamp of faith at the unwavering flame
Burnt for the altar service of the Race
Since the beginning. He shall find the strange—
The white immaculate Virgin of the North,
Whose steady gaze no mortal ever dared,
Whose icy hand no human ever grasped.
In the dread silence and the solitude
She waits and listens through the centuries
For one indomitable, destined soul,
Born to endure the glory of her eyes,
And lift his warm lips to the frozen Grail.

THE SONG OF THE NORTH POLE FLAG

I AM the banner of earth's farthest goal!
Can any gaze on me and doubt Man's soul
  Is mightier than the armies of despair,
And older than the Star that guards the Pole?

The youngest of all banners, I have made
The loneliest journeys, glad and unafraid;
  I know the crags where hungry horrors crawl
And with the wild wind demons I have played.

Love made me in the smiling earlier years;
But I was cut with Destiny's cold shears
  From fabrics woven on Fame's iron loom,
And I am stained with time, with sweat, and tears.

In the beginning I was meant to be
Only the nation's emblem; then round me
  New meanings were assembled, and I stand
Now as the ensign of Man's sovereignty.

For every star—some stab of adverse Fate;
My crimson stripes are bands of love and hate
  That have been loosened, and my field of blue
Is the long Northern night wherein we wait.

Then gaze upon my wounds. For I have left
Fragments of me in many an ice-fringed cleft;
   Marking the desperate highway step by step
Are Glory's shrines—and portions of my weft.

At last I waved on earth's last mound of white,
And triumphed in the radiant, frosty light;
   For only he who leaves himself behind
Shall stand with God upon the utmost height.

FREEDOM

CALL no man free nor count his bondage done,
    Though he be master of unminted gold
  With kings to do him homage, if his hold
Be not so strong on the immortal sun—
The shining, heliocentric Self—that none
    May loosen it. Fearless and will-controlled,
    Alike though friends pursue him or grow cold—
That man the crown of liberty has won.

And fancy not that feeling, and the thrill
    Of love, are absent from him. Infinite
The love that waits the calling of his will
    Whose longing is the whole world's benefit;
And happiness shall flood him to the fill—
    When he has mastered the desire of it.

ONE OF THESE LITTLE ONES

O LITTLE child, O wide-eyed wondering child!
  Well do I know you are a captured wild
Bird from the outer blue, that beats its wings
Against the barriers of earth-bound things.
How many miles into the awful vast
Your mother must have soared, to seize you fast
And bring you back with her, to be a white
Proof of the fearless journey! The sunlight
Still half bewilders you; and in your sleep
You smile, because the darkness is so deep
After the earth-glare, and the rest so kind
After the search for One you cannot find.

You are the Dream made flesh. You are the grail
Pilgrim,—another, passionate and frail,
Leaving the House of Beauty for the quest
Of that high Vision by no man possessed.
Indomitable must be God's desire
To realise Life's secret and acquire
Mastery, when he sends you, one by one,
Eternally, to question the bright sun
And the dark earth and the indifferent stars!
O Baby! will you pass the golden bars

Guarding the pathway to the great abode?
Or will you leave your dust to make the road
Softer for those who follow? I am blind,
Even as Love or Justice, and I find
No answer to the riddle that has wrung
The souls of mothers since the world was **young.**

THE DREAMERS

WHAT matter though the thorn of pain
　　Forever seeks our quivering heart,
And midnight of our tears is fain?
Our sorrows are the golden grain
　　Of the great reaper—Art.

What matter though we ask for bread,
　　And the dull world bestows the stone?
On God's own manna we are fed,
Honey of dreams, and wine love-red
　　To the dull world unknown.

Earth's palace doors are open wide
　.　That narrow souls may enter in;
But we in Beauty's tent abide,
Adoring that unravished bride
　　Whose veil the ages spin.

We walk the vision-haunted way
　　Beyond the rainbow's fragile bridge;
In Uriel's inner shrine we pray;
With equal wonder we survey
　　The planet and the midge.

THE FROZEN GRAIL

The Rose of Life to us reveals
  Her hidden petals without shame,
For in our questing faith she feels
The love that melts the seven seals
  Of the Eternal Name.

BEFORE DAWN

WHEN in the lone and silence of the night
    I wake bewildered with desire and dread,—
Peering among the shadows round my bed
For something that eludes me in the light,—
I hearken for those echoes from the height
    That thrilled the dreams still hovering overhead,
    In that dim land where longing lures the dead
To lend our earth-blind eyes their clearer sight.

Then, then for one brief heartbeat there appears
    To me the vision of my austere soul,
    Godlike and pure, with storied aureole,
And eyes that burn with memories of lost years,
    And finger pointing my forsaken goal . . .
Oh, hide me, God, in the blind deep of tears!

THE MUSE

SHE is the idol of the wise,
  The mistress of the rhyming race;
But pain lurks in her luring eyes,
  And bitter-sweet is her embrace.

She lightly chains her chosen ones
  With whispered secrets, half-confessed;
But when they summon her, she shuns
  And leaves them to the lonely quest.

The face of love is not so fair
  As hers; all tender questionings
And dreams are hidden in her hair,
  And memories of forgotten things.

The siren of the sea of souls,
  She lures her lovers with the lyre
To leave their galleys for the goals
  Where burns the sacrificial fire.

The world and all the wealth of it
  They barter for her lightning kiss—
The rhythm of the Infinite,
  The vision of the vast abyss.

But they who drink the Muse's breath
  Pay for the draught with many tears—
Their destiny until their death
  To seek her shadow down the years.

Sometimes into their lone retreat
  Is blown her veil's divine perfume;
Sometimes her rainbow-sandalled feet
  Go whispering by them in the gloom.

And strange and varied gifts she brings:
  To some the amaranth of fame,
To some the gaunt wolf's yammerings,
  To some the burning book of shame.

Along the lanes of alien lands
  Their hard and lonely pathway lies,
And not a being understands
  The wistful madness of their eyes.

Sometimes, when twilight veils the street,
  A wanderer hears upon the air
A sound so mystically sweet,
  He sighs a half-forgotten prayer;

Sometimes the whole world starts, and thrills
  To harmonies that vastly roll . . .
'Tis only one of them who stills
  With song the yearning of his soul.

THROUGH THE VEIL

ALWAYS it seems
    That only a thin veil—
  Sheer as the music of the nightingale—
Trembles and streams
Between me and the mystery of dreams.

Sometimes at dawn,
  I am so strangely near
  I feel its high, ecstatic atmosphere.
And then . . . 'tis gone!
A breath stirs, and the wonder is withdrawn.

Sometimes a bird
  Sings at the twilight hour,
  Or I perceive the fragrance of a flower . . .
And I have heard,
But cannot speak, the unapparent word.

Sometimes the breeze
  Passes over my hair
  Like the hand of Something . . . and I turn and stare . . .
And my soul sees
A fluttering in the sensitive willow trees!

But oftener,
   When I am very still,
   Deep in my heart I feel a sudden thrill:
A messenger
From the Unseen signals and would confer.

Some day, I know,
   That Presence will appear—
   Too high to reach, too beautiful to fear!
My songs I owe
To a strange sign it made me long ago.

THE CONQUEROR

WHAT are the fears and toils of life to me,
  That I should tremble on my guarded throne
Or plead for pity, making human moan
Like any helpless creature! Verily
The crown is to the conqueror, and I see
  Beyond this hour of battle. I have sown
  With lavish hand my fertile fields, and own
The plenty of my harvests. Destiny,
Tyrant of slaves, is servant of my will;
  To all my gods are her libations poured,
And only at my bidding may she fill
  The cups of good and evil on my board.
My song Time's warning finger shall not still,
  Nor Pain destroy me with his flaming sword!

THE SERVANTS OF THE KING

ONE day I wandered out upon the road
   That spans the mad world, near my calm abode,
 Seeking companions in the restless throng
That staggered on beneath its varied load.

I bore no burden, save a rhymester's pack
That lay as light as wings upon my back;
 My goal was life, my only task to sing
And speed the sun round the glad Zodiac.

I hailed a haggard fellow with a pile
Of printed stuff—the world's ephemeral file,
 Calling, " Come, listen to a troubadour ! "
He said, " I may have time—after a while."

There passed another in a gorgeous dress,
Laden with gems, but pale with weariness.
 " Pause, friend," I smiled, " and listen to the wind."
" Pause ! " he replied, " and lose all I possess ? "

Then came a man with bricks upon his head,
Pursuing blindly his elusive bread.
 I called, " Come, listen to a song of life ! "
" What is a song? And what is life ? " he said.

THE FROZEN GRAIL

I cried, "What seek ye all—what wondrous thing!—
That ye have time neither to laugh nor sing,
   Nor hearts to love, nor hours to think, or dream?"
They said, "We do not know: we serve the king."

"Who is the king to whom your lives are sold?
What means his power?" I questioned young and old,
   Seeking for knowledge; and I only heard:
"The king is nameless; but his power is gold."

I cried, "Your king is mad! Why, if he knew
The test that separates the false and true,—
   That sifts life's kernel from its worthless chaff,—
Would he not, find some nobler use for you?"

THE MIDNIGHT LUNCH ROOM

WITH little silver one may enter here,
   And yet those hungry faces watch outside
The frosty window—and the door is wide!
The clatter to my unaccustomed ear
Of dishes and harsh tongues, is like a spear
 ˙Shaken within the sensitive wounded side
   Of Silence. Soiled, indifferent hands provide
Pitiful fare, and cups of pallid cheer.

In my warm, fragrant home an hour ago
   I wrote a sonnet on the peace they win
Who worship Beauty! Let me breathe it low . . .
   What would it mean if chanted in this din?
What would it say to those out in the snow,
   Who hunger, and who may not enter in?

POET-BROTHER

BEAUTIFUL Brother, with the wild thrush note
That soars and thrills—and catches in your throat
With rain of tones and tears! Do you recall
How shadow-lyrics flickered on the wall,
Back in Euterpe's palace of star-snow
And deathless roses, in the long ago?
Babes of that gentle mother, from her breast
Drawing the milk of wonder, we were blest
With rhythmic sustenance, made pure and strong
In the high-born fraternity of song.

Nay, do you wonder we are aliens here
With the earth-people? We have been too near,
Brother of mine, to the pale moon of dreams
Ever to measure how unreal it seems
To those who love the gaslight. We have heard
The far-off singing of the homeless bird—
Whose name is Beauty; but the world of men,
Busy with cares, will hardly listen when
Our trembling reverent lips repeat the song.
Pilgrims of time are we, and overlong
Seems the great quest. The mystery of tears
Our souls have tasted; but the listening years
Will learn a new, glad music through our breath
Before we lie in the loving arms of Death.

Beautiful elder brother, in the cold
Desert of hope my spirit is consoled
By your strong hand-clasp. Though we wander **far**
Each from the other, though the future bar
The doors of life between us; yet I know
That I shall find you where the lilies blow
Around the mystic fountain. I shall stand
Singing beside you on the silver sand
Of the Uranian ocean. And my faith,
Beckoning afar, shall call you as a wraith
Over the shadows, when the demons lean
And lure you from the crags of the Unseen.

A BOOK OF MAGIC

OLD learnèd reveller in mystic joys
    And darer of the demons! I have read
Your symbol-graven pages full of dread—
Of godlike exaltation. Childish toys,
Circles and wheels, your subtle hand employs
    To more than mature uses. Were the dead
    Indeed your servants? Have the unborn fled
Before your word, that raises or destroys?

I have a magic higher far than yours,
    Marvellous *Lévi*,* and its works are signed
With God's own seal: The patient love that çures
    All the lone, bitter sadness of the mind;
The gentle word that comforts and endures;
    The faith that lights a beacon for mankind.

*Eliphas Lévi: *"Haute Magie."*

29

THE MASTER OF PAIN

MASTER with the patient eyes,
  Thou art pitiful and wise;
In the folds of thy red garment
Hush my broken cries.

Dost thou hold me then so dear,
Master, in thy heart austere,
  That I never can escape thee
For one little year?

Let my yearning soul enjoy
Peace and love without alloy
  For one brief but golden season—
Thou canst yet destroy!

Pity me—as thou art strong!
Leave me in the fields of song;
  I would linger in the sunshine,
For the night is long.

Thou wilt promise unto me
If I wrest my spirit free,
  Power and treasure beyond measure,
As my stars decree;

THE FROZEN GRAIL

If I drink thy bitter-sweet,
Bind thy sandals on my feet,
  Thou wilt lead me through Pain's **valley**
Unto peace complete.

I may stand with thee at last
Where the present and the past
  And the future blend together
In the timeless Vast;

Where the singing of the spheres
Charms away all human fears,
  And the harps of unborn beings
Echo down the years.

There the passions of the earth
Will appear of little worth,
  And my soul will scarce remember
Its own tears and mirth.

AFTER FIFTEEN YEARS

THE hills are not so high as once they were;
    And the old woods, that seemed so dark and vast
  In those remembered child days of the past,
Are only a few trees, that now confer
In whispers of this curious wayfarer
  Who stands and gazes so. The young pines cast
  Shy glances at me; they were twigs when last
I questioned them, and they were tenderer.

The grey old empty house is like a dream
  That haunts the memory in the clear noonday.
  The silent room of birth is tenanted
By disembodied yearnings, and they seem
  Vaguely to know that I have found a way
  To something unimagined by the dead.

MARIE

OH, why is your merry laugh, Marie,
    Made strange by an under sound?
It haunts my heart like the memory
    Of a face I have never found.
'Tis maybe you hear the crying drear
    Of my baby underground.

Why flows the golden wine, Marie,
    So freely for your sake?
Can you drink of its joy so feverishly
    With never an after ache?
'Tis my thirst from the tears I have drunk long years
    No cup can ever slake.

And why do you dance and sing, Marie,
    Till the call of the wakening lark,
Till the morning star nods drowsily
    And is only a smouldering spark?
I'm the lamp at the head of his lonely bed,
    For I know he fears the dark.

And why when the laughter is gay, Marie,
    And the midnight minutes fly,
Do you clutch your breast all suddenly,
    With a gasp and a startled cry?
'Tis the biting drought of his cold, small mouth,
    That will hurt me till I die.

35

ON A BUNDLE OF NEW POETS

THEY are so many who in early spring
   Gather the wild wood violets of song
To weave a wreath for Beauty! They are strong
With untried sinews, and the Vision's wing
Has brushed their souls in passing. Shadows cling
   Around them in the noonday, and the long
   Reaches of night are peopled with a throng
Of laurelled phantoms, gravely beckoning.

They are so few, so few who find the shrine
   Of the white Wonder! For the air is cold
Upon the mount of triumph, and malign
   Dragons beset the path. Only the bold
May dare the love that makes man's words divine—
   The faith that fired the prophet bards of old.

THE QUEST

ONE thing I know, if only one:
  Before Life's glowing west
Shall swallow up my setting sun,
  My soul will end its quest.

Hard are the roads and hazardous,
  But sure my soul's designs;
The Moon and mystic Uranus
  Have sealed them in the Signs.

I know not if the treasure sought
  Be love, or God, or death;
But that my title has been wrought
  Of passion, blood and breath.

Somewhere I know the wonder waits;
  And though the days are long,
I challenge the stern, bloodless Fates
  To still my calling-song.

But I have found strange company:
  Aye, in the maze of years
My mind has known the madman's glee,
  I have tasted gall and tears.

THE FROZEN GRAIL

For I have dared to grasp my dreams,
  Though knowing they were null;
Have dared to face the light that gleams
  Upon the hollow skull.

Yet, God, thou knowest I am weak
  And weary, and would rest.
Unveil the symbol that I seek—
  The Sangreal of my quest!

THE COUNSELLORS

MY soul was taking counsel with my mind
    Last night when all the city lay asleep.
  The mind said:—Sister, wherefore dost thou weep,
Now when the world is willing to be kind
To our divine endeavour? Though we find
    The pathway up the mountain wild and steep,
    Surely we will not stumble if we keep
Bravely together with our arms entwined.

But softly the soul answered through her tears:—
    The kindness of the world is like a vine,
Sister, whose intricate network interferes
    With the soul's climbing. Yonder summit shrine
He never reaches who too fondly peers
    Into the foaming goblet of world-wine.

REQUIESCAT

WHY do you cry so loudly underground,
 Buried Ideal? Have I not laid you deep,
 And drugged you with grim truths to make you sleep,
And set the cross above your low, bare mound?

You were the last of all my rainbow band!
 For years I hid you in a guarded place,
 That none might see your sweet, unearthly face,
Nor hear your words no brain could understand.

Even to you has come the destined hour
 That waits for all things lovely. On your brow
 I laid my lips in parting, to walk now
The lone unfriended alien path of power.

Why do you haunt me still with yearning cries?
 Long have you stood between me and the goal
 Only discovered by the clear-eyed soul
That dares the face of Life without disguise.

Never again till cold earth covers me
 Can you and I hold counsel the night through.
 Never again shall I deny for you
What all the mocking gods declare to be.

DANTE

PALE Priest of Song, immortal as the earth
   That walks the skies with pride, remembering thee!
  Deign to receive, from my humility,
One word to swell the story of thy worth
Kept in the world's great archives. At thy birth
  The stars of Fame's nine heavens auspiciously
  Assembled, and the sun of Poetry,
Blazing too fiercely, made thy life a dearth.

But oh, the glory and beatitude,
  When thine ecstatic vision, justified
    By flaming song, made heaven forever real!
So, Master, we thy scholars, poor and crude,
  Now follow thee, as thou thy laurelled guide,
    Up the steep road to our divine Ideal.

BESIDE THE ROAD

FROM my still cottage, off the road,
  I see the noisy world go by,
Forever driven by the goad,
Forever bending to the load,
  Unmindful of the sky.

The spring is here—to-day I found
  A bed of golden daffodils.
I passed the dull throng blossom-crowned;
But could not make them turn around,
  Nor join me on the hills.

I know a bank beneath the trees
  Where fragrant purple violets blow;
I plucked the fairest, on my knees;
Their fresh, cool beauty seemed to please
  Those plodding ones below.

But when I beckoned toward the wood,
  They did not turn and follow me;
Yet by their eyes I understood
They longed to gather flowers, and would—
  If they were only free.

47

But, oh, it is not always spring!
  Winter, that smites all blossoms dead,
Will find my throng still labouring
Toward the same hollow, useless Thing—
  But youth and passion fled!

TO THE APOLLO BELVEDERE

O POET'S vision, petrified by art
In those glad days when Song was deified,
Before the simple joy of nature died,
Or man was burdened with a contrite heart!
From the dull rabble of our modern mart
I turn to thee, high being, justified
In everlasting beauty, passion, pride!
In our cold age thou hast no counterpart.

Glorious Apollo! Little now remains
To prove our plodding race was ever young,
That once man's blood flowed freely in his veins,
That out of sheer delight he loved and sung.
When now a lyric measure thrills his tongue,
'Tis mainly to bewail his hidden pains.

49

THE VISIT OF THE MUSE

BEING, that comes to me out of the night,
   Walking the moonbeams all silvery-white,
What is the message you bid me to write?

Are you the Muse whom the rhymers of old
Saw in their visions, but never could hold—
She whose rare boons are not bartered and sold?

Long have I wondered when you would appear!
But, in my garret so bare and austere,
Muse, I have naught for your comfort, I fear,—

Only a cot with a rose at its head,
A board that is richer in books than in bread,
A taper whose flame on the future is fed.

Am I too bold, that I beg you to stay?
Leisure is costly, and this is the way
Poets have lived since the myth-makers' day.

We are so happy with fancies and rhymes.
What do we need of the toys of the times—
We who in visions can visit all climes?

You that are waiting with 'largess for me,
Give me the words of a song that shall be
Hope for the bond and a spur for the free!

Give me a song of the love that shall bind,
Even as comrades, the mass of Mankind—
Song of the guerdon they seeking shall find.

Burn me, O Muse, with your mystical flame!
Whisper the sounds of Man's unified name,
And I will relinquish the prizes of fame.

Give me the music my brothers will sing
In the joy of the morning when Love shall be king . . .
Then bury me under the daisies of spring.

THE SOUL OF ART

I LISTEN to the rhymers' praise of art,
   Of the immortal form, the measured phrase;
  Of the one mirror, and the many ways
The poet's pale reflection to impart:
But not a word of the initiate heart,
   Of the incarnate Light whose subtle blaze,
   Intimate of the soul, eludes the gaze—
Man's goal of yearning, and his counterpart.

I, too, am learnèd in the lore of sound,
   In the cold measurement of lyric speech;
But what availed my knowledge, till I found
   The hidden Thing mere art can never teach,
The selfless Thing, too great to be renowned,
   So high—it is within the lowest reach!

VISHNU, THE PERVADER

I AM the self in the centre of all things; I am the un-
known
Wind-swept void on the perilous far outside of my own
Self;
I am the darkness of night, and the mystery under the
shadows;
I am the vision of light in the love-dazzled eyes of the sun.

I am the ache of desire in the burning caress of the lover;
Mine is the yearning that draws, and the yielding of love
in the loved one;
I am the soul that gives, and the gift, and the joy of the
giving;
I am the quiver of hope in the heart of the mother of men.

All earth's musical sounds are but echoes that answer my
piping;
Mine is the voice of the thunder, mine is the coo of the
ring-dove;
I am the murmur of waters, the whispering wind in the
pine-trees;
I am the word in the silence, the dread, and the listening
hush.

I am the ecstasy found in the sleep that no mortal remembers.

Mine are all creatures that crawl, or aspire, or await their aspiring;

Even the writhe of the worm is his longing endeavour to reach Me;

The cry of the eagle is torn from his heart at my touch in the cold air.

THE DWELLER

I MEDITATE upon the soul within.
    Mysterious dweller, could I comprehend
  The need of thy beginning, and the end
Of all thy struggles! Does the school of Sin
(So named on earth) provide the discipline
  Thy subtle wisdom seeks—the guide and friend,
  Garbed as a foe, whose conquest shall transcend
In power all thy lost innocence might win?

Sages have written of thee; but the word—
  If there be one—that can reveal thy deep,
  Deliberate purpose, still designs to keep
Its boon, for all my pleading, unconferred.
Yet puzzling counsels have I overheard
  Sometimes on the unguarded winds of sleep.

THE EXILE

O COOL, still woods and smiling sky!
  God's home of green and blue!
When will the world have done with me
  And send me back to you?

The noises of the restless town—
  Jarring, importunate—
Can never drown the memory
  Of whispering pines that wait.

Oh, will they really wait for me?
  So long I am away!
Sometimes I fear the laggard years
  May, after all, betray.

It would be very hard to die
  Here in the dust and roar,
And never feel the cool, still woods
  Around me any more!

THE ALIEN SINGER

INFINITUDE of distance lies between
   Your world and mine, dear Stranger, though
      your hand
  Lies in my palm so kindly; for the land
I dwell in, is the land of the Unseen.
And though I sing its beauty, what I mean
   You know not, neither do you understand;
   Even the language of our peaceful band
Sounds strange in your loud, turbulent demesne.

But we who wander alien on the earth,
   Return in dream to our beloved home
   Beyond the crags of silence. There we roam
The gardens of the stars that ruled our birth;
And with our song, from elemental dearth
   Create your future's walls and splendid dome.

TWO FRIENDS

THE sweet friend of my body said to me:
　　"Come to the garden, dear,
And gather roses while the days are clear;
For bye and bye 'twill be
　　The blossomless grey autumn of the year."

The stern friend of my spirit said to me:
　　"Daughter, thy way lies here—
Here where the flint path leads up to the clear
Height of Eternity,
　　On the Soul's mountain, passionless, austere."

And I? . . . I stood between them silently
　　And wiped away a tear;
　　For well I knew the flowers would disappear,
The summer fade for me . . .
　　And yet the flint path filled my soul with fear!

IN THE MIRROR

I HOLD life's magic mirror in my hand,
   And gaze in my own eyes that meet me there
   Fearlessly. Sister, passion and despair
Have set their seals upon thee; but our grand
Indomitable spirit still doth stand
   Steadfast amid the tumult. Thou dost wear
   Mysteries hidden in thy midnight hair
Beyond my power ever to understand.

O thou flower-soft and rosy woman-form
   That our stern spirit chose to test life through!
   Come, let us laugh together as we view
The little fears and hates that feebly swarm
Around our dwelling—safe in every storm
   If to each other thou and I are true.

PRAYER

MASTER and Maker of the suns and seas,
　　Thou in whose hand the ripening ages fall!
I raise my feeble voice in praise of Thee—
But when hadst Thou the need of mortal praise?
Whether I cry to Thee as a loving God,
And bring in prayer to Thee my petty griefs,
My keen desires, important as the moth's;
Or in the silence of the mystic night—
The solemn silence of Thy sentient stars—
I dumbly worship Thee as the Unknown God,
My word can bring Thee nothing that shall add
Aught to Thine ancient glory. Yet, sometimes,
When I forget Thee in the rush of song
That sweeps my rapt soul out beyond all reverence . . .
For one swift heart-leap do I feel Thy breath
In awful benediction on my brow.

KEATS

HYPERION of poets . . . Shining one!
   To thy pavilion in the realm of air
  Can my soul's incense rise? Art thou aware
Thy name in every singer's orison
Is writ in stars, not water? Has there none
  Of all earth's dying dreamers scaled the stair
  Of light after thee, breathless to declare
Even to thy face thy fame beneath the sun?

But maybe in the region where thou art
  No rumour of the world or the world's ways
Can ever come. Thy dreams are now a part
  Of God's own vision, and thy deathless lays
Signed with His name. Approved by Him, thy heart
  Is all oblivious of human praise.

THE POET

HE who is born with the vision of beauty,
  The veil of dream,
Has one supreme and mystical duty—
  To shed the gleam
  Of his fortunate star on the world's grey stream.

Always the seraphs are winging and singing,
  Though few can hear
The rapturous music the winds are bringing.—
  Thou keen of ear,
  Translate their songs for our denser sphere.

Poet, thy joy is the whole world's treasure,
  Not thine alone.
Thy soul is an overflowing measure
  Of seed to be sown
  In the yearning soil of this alien zone.

INVOCATION

MUSE, I have served thee now untiringly
    For seven years . . . Unveil thy hidden face!
  Here at the measure of my term of grace
Give me thy boon, the benedicite
My spirit trembles toward. Thy veil I see
    Over the world in spring, and shimmering space
    Is dizzy with thee, and thy wild embrace
Beckons me in the thrill of poetry.

Oh, search my spirit with thy cryptic eyes!
  I am all thine; accept my service now,
  And seal my purposes. Anoint my brow
With thy protecting chrism: A singer dies
So soon—sometimes before he justifies
  The faith of his inviolable vow!

TWO MEN OF OLD

TO live and love and sing sweet songs
   Was all the Poet sought;
His robe was threadbare, but he wore
   The diadem of thought;
The plodders blamed his dreamy ways,
   Nor knew what he had wrought.

The Statesman schemed and gave his wealth
   To buy immortal fame;
The Emperor of half the world
   To grace his banquets came;
And many little busy men
   Were noisy with his name.

A thousand years of days and nights,
   And names, have rolled away:
The Statesman's proud, ephemeral fame
   Sleeps with his nameless clay;
But the little songs the poet sang
   The whole world loves to-day.

OSCAR WILDE

LAUREATE of corruption, on whose brow
The bay-leaves are all slimy with the worm!
Thou art a nightingale whose songs affirm
The canker in the rosebud, from a bough
Of the dark cypress warbling. Some strange vow
Thy spirit must have taken before birth
To some strange god, to desecrate the earth
With visions vile and beautiful as thou.

We loathe thee with the sure, instinctive dread
Of young things for the graveyard and the scar.
And though God wept when Lucifer's great star
With its long train cried from the deeps blood-red,
Still must we name thee with the second dead,
For when the angels fall they fall so far!

THE ANGEL OF THE SEPULCHRE

KNOW ye that every Resurrection morn
    The Angel of the Sepulchre comes down
To the world tomb where slumbering souls lie low,
And rolls away the stone that guards the door?
Thus the great Angel came to me at dawn
This Easter Sunday, calling to my soul
That had been crucified by the mad world,
Broken and buried—was it days ago,
Or ages that the temple veil was rent?

Whoever has beheld that Angel's face
Has felt the dead Christ rising in his heart
And throwing off the grave-clothes. Till that day,
The lips of men may chant at Eastertime
The glory of the Lord they say is risen;
But all their words are only flickering lights
Thrown by the rising sun into their tomb,
Through some slight crevice in the door of clay.

THE SEEKER

WHAT is the guerdon that my soul has sought
    Blindly my life long over land and sea?
Morning and evening does it beckon me,
And in the blaze of noon's laborious thought.
But though I ever follow, I have caught
    Only the phantom hands of Mystery
    Death-cold; and from my dreams of ecstasy
I wake—to face the omnipresent Naught.

Spirit of mine, thy strength will never tire;
    Yet would I know what means thy pathless quest,
Would know the goal of thy long, vague desire.
    What guide of destiny unmanifest
So lures thee on with cloud and pillared fire
    Through the dark wilderness of life's unrest?

THE EASTER CHILDREN

" CHRIST the Lord is risen! "
      Chant the Easter children,
Their love-moulded faces
Luminous with gladness,
And their costly raiment
Gleaming like the lilies.

But last night I wandered
Where Christ had not risen,
Where love knows no gladness,
Where the lord of Hunger
Leaves no room for lilies,
And no time for childhood.

And to-day I wonder
Whether I am dreaming;
For above the swelling
Of their Easter music
I can hear the murmur,
" Suffer *all* the children."

Nay, the world is dreaming!
And my seeing spirit
Trembles for its waking,
When their Saviour rises
To restore the lilies
To the outcast children.

THE GERMAN IMMIGRANTS

HERE to the home where past and future meet,
   By myriads you have come, your wistful hearts
  Aflame with hope. You traffic in the marts,
And with the very mortar of the street
Mix your high dreams. Your fields of waving wheat
  Banner the West; your tireless mining starts
· The fires of nations; while our new world arts
Owe to the land of Faust and Marguerite
Treasures of virile beauty. Brain and brawn,
  O Rhineland! have you given us, and profound
  Are your seed-thoughts sown in our mental ground.
Your son was he who hailed the social dawn;
Your sons were they whose harmonies have drawn
  Our new-born music from the caves of sound.

SONG OF THE ITALIAN IMMIGRANTS

FROM Rome are we, and Genoa,
    And the warm southern vinelands, too;
Naples and all Italia
Remember us in dreams . . . but, ah!
    Our hearts have chosen you,

Great unknown country over-seas,
    America! Will you deny
Our prayer? or raise us from our knees,
With leave to labour as the bees
    All day without a sigh?

Italia's sons no toils dismay:
    We raised the Colosseum's wall,
We laid the peerless Appian way
Never to crumble till the day
    When all old things shall fall.

We are Colombo's kindred; we
    Follow the star that lured him far
To find thy cradle in the sea,—
Light of the world, Land of the free!
    Unbar thy doors, unbar!

NEW YORK HARBOUR AT NIGHT

THE magic veil of night is on the bay.
 Beneath its starry folds the waters glow—
 A floor of lapis-lazuli below;
The lights along the shores, a girdle gay
Of many-coloured jewels, gleaming play;
 In the far west the little moon hangs low;
 While from yon dusky form the torch's glow
Tells where our sleepless guardian stands for aye.

City of mine—lovely by day, by night!
 Like Venus, you have risen from the sea,
  That holds your dear feet still in tender grasp;
Like Venus, you have won by fair decree
 Your beauty's million-jewelled girdle bright,
  Held round you by the Bridge's diamond clasp.

THE BUILDER

ONLY the Dreamer builds to challenge Time,
    Whether he builds a state, or builds a rhyme;
  The vision of his midnight greets the day
In Beauty's form—imperishable, sublime.

THE INVADERS

STRANGE is that timeless battle for the world
Which poets wage! Their destiny it is
To lead invasions down the centuries,
Beyond the outposts of that realm whose purled
And lilied banner God Himself unfurled
In the beginning; for no realm of His
He guards like that of Beauty. Ecstasies
Against their souls, like passionate armies hurled,
Still drive them back when they approach too near,
Smiting them prostrate if they do not fly
The fiery onslaught. Should the world deny
Their humble soldier-wages, then they cheer
Each other with their songs, and disappear
Down the long winding roads of the bye-and-bye.

THE WORD OF SUMMER

DROPPING roses from her hand,
  Came dear Summer down the land,
  With her hair a tawny banner
By the breezes fanned.

And she looked and laughed at me,
Where I sat all mournfully,
  Counting over my lost labours,
Near a cypress tree.

And she said: "Oh! why repine?
All these patient works of mine—
  Leaves and flowers and fragrant apples—
I must soon resign.

"Not one blossom will remain!
But do I, like thee, complain?
  Nay, I pause and rest a season,
Then begin again."

MY GOLDEN SANDS

TO-DAY I meditate upon the years
  Whose sands have fallen in the glass of Time
Since I was flung into this foreign clime
Out of infinitude.   And it appears
The one reward of pleasure and of tears
  Is always knowledge; that the paradigm
  Whereon my life was modelled, is sublime
Experience, beyond all woman fears.

And though my precious grains of golden sand
  Have dropped this first faint signal on my hair,
  I would not count them backward.   And I swear
Each as it falls shall leave at my demand
Some treasure of the Spirit in my hand—
  And take no bauble that I would not spare!

MAGDALENA

"I HAVE seen the Master's face
Bending down to my low place—
    Seen his eyes of boundless pity
Proving my disgrace.

"And I follow at his side,
Though He knows all I would hide—
    All the burning love I could not
Smother if I tried."

THE VIGIL OF JOSEPH

AFTER the Wise Men went, and the strange star
Had faded out, Joseph the father sat
Watching the sleeping Mother and the Babe,
And thinking stern, sweet thoughts the long night through.

"Ah, what am I, that God has chosen me
To bear this blessed burden, to endure
Daily the presence of this loveliness,
To guide this Glory that shall guide the world?

"Brawny these arms to win Him bread, and broad
This bosom to sustain Her. But my heart
Quivers in lonely pain before that Beauty
It loves—and serves—and cannot understand!"

COME TO ME, LITTLE ONE

COME to me, little one, drowsy and dear;
  Mother will spare me her darling awhile.
I am so lonely when twilight is here!
  Lie on my bosom, and nestle, and smile.

I have no little one, dearie, like you,
  No little hand to hold close in the night,
No one to dream of the lonely hours through,
  No one to wake for when God sends the light.

You are so sorry? Oh, bless you, my sweet!
  Dear little fingers that wipe off the tears!
Little soft body and little white feet,
  How will they treat you—the terrible years?

Life is so fair to a baby like you;
  All things are wonderful under the sun,
Rainbows are real, and all stories are true.—
  Would they might be so when childhood is done!

Wide little eyes that are questioning so,
  Life is no stranger to you than to me.
The secrets worth knowing I never shall know,
  The end of the rainbow I never shall see.

THE FROZEN GRAIL

So, little drowsy one, nestle and sleep,—
  Lullaby, baby, O lullaby-low!
There always is peace in the dreams that are deep,—
  Lullaby, little one, lullaby-low.

THE MOSQUITO

THE slime has taken wings, and cries to me
    To feed its fury with my finer life;
So full of the intense desire *to be*
    Is each earth atom, and so fierce the strife!

THE VISITOR

CROSS the city roofs it came,
  A golden butterfly,
Into my open window here—
  So bare and grey and high!

Unmindful of my startled gaze,
  It hovered overhead;
Then lit beside the crèpen veil
  Which lay upon the bed.

Only a moment did it stay
  Beside the symbol there;
Its golden wings it spread again
  And vanished in the air.

How strange that such a visitor
  Should seek this granite height!—
Or was it the bewildered soul
  Of her who died last night?

THE HAUNTER OF THE TWILIGHT

WHERE are you now, as the night draws down,
    Comrade of mine?
I have followed you out of the noisy town
To a narrow house, all bare and brown,
    And left you lonely and supine,
    Without a sign.

Three long days did I question you
    When none was nigh.
Three long nights did my soul pursue
Your fleeing soul, for a final clue
    To the mystic errand, swift and high,
    That made you die.

Side by side we were sitting there
    At dusk of day.
Though nearer the door, I was not aware
When the chilly Stranger passed my chair.
    I could not hear what you turned to say
    As you went away.

Comrade of mine, was the secret sweet
    The Stranger taught—
A message of triumph to charm defeat,
Giving you joy of your last heartbeat?
    You went so quickly he must have brought
    The thing you sought.

Then why I am troubled as night draws near
  With a vague unrest? . . .
It is not hope, it is not fear,
But I feel an uneasy presence here;
  And I know for the souls who have entered the West,
  Deep sleep is best.

PENITENCE

OH, bitter are the penitential tears
    That water the Tree of Knowledge! Could I grasp
  Tightly the subtil serpent, till no gasp
Of life were left in that lithe form that rears
Its jewelled head to mock me, my proud years
  Would wear the achievement as a diamond clasp.
  But under every rose-tree the coiled asp
Waits with its message for my willing ears.

"Stay thy rash hand!" the great Voice counsels me.
  "Knowest thou not the Teacher, foolish one?
Study the strange new lesson given thee.
  Waste not thine hour regretting what is done.
Thou knowest much that still was mystery
  Ere thy regretful tears darkened the sun."

ON LAKE GEORGE

BECALMED within my little boat I lie,
  Between the night lake and the star-eyed sky,
And all the spellbound Universe is I.

My dark doubt is the cloud on yonder height,
My faith—the peace that hovers on the night,
My lives—the myriad rays of the starlight.

I am these yearning spheres of sky and earth;
My thought encircles their stupendous girth
As light encircled us before our birth.

One, in the womb of Life, did we remain
Through ages unrecorded; and God's gain
Was great the day we were brought forth in pain.

But suddenly my boat rocks in the wind!
Madly the lake reels—like a wayward mind,
And all the eyes of night are stricken blind.

The cloud from yonder height obscures all things:
The peace that hovered, now beats frightened wings,
And my lone life to her lone body clings.

Now, on the sea of Time, only a mark
Am I; my form is the frail tossing barque
Between me and the void and timeless dark.

THE GUARDIANS

THERE is a beauty in the faded leaves
   That lie all disregarded on the ground;
The guardians of the blossom and the fruit
   In those dry forms are found.

And there is beauty in the faded men—
   The disregarded on life's toilsome ways;
Their blood has fed the blossom of our songs,
   And theirs should be the praise.

A   WORD

I BREATHED a little word all heedlessly
   One cloudy morning to a doubting friend,
  A word whose deeps I did not comprehend,
A word of wonder and of destiny.
'Twas long ago; but still those sounds to me
  Re-echo, and their burden will extend
  In broken rhythm beyond time's faint end,
Marring the stillness of eternity.

So now I stand with wide and watchful eyes,
  And ever-guarding finger on my lip,
  That from my heart no heedless word may slip—
No subtle word for doubt to signalise.
Something is wrong with man, if, to be wise,
  He must forego freedom in fellowship!

REALISATION

HE gazed indifferently across the wide
   Home river mirroring the infinite sky.
"Oh, to behold Jerusalem!" he cried.
   "To bathe in Jordan river ere I die!"

As an earthworm that restlessly inquires
   The road to daylight, reaches the sun's beams,
So he at last came to his heart's desire—
   Came to the city and river of his dreams.

Jerusalem the Mighty was now spread
   Before him . . . He was homesick and forlorn.
"Why, 'tis not half so beautiful," he said,
   "As the elm-shaded town where I was born!"

He bathed in Jordan river . . . It was cold.
   Was this the storied stream that he had sought?
"Oh, how the books deceived me! Why, the old
   River at home is twice as wide!" he thought.

THE OFFERING

SOUL of the Universe, to Thee I bring
    Tribute of all my treasures, and entreat
  Only Thy full acceptance. At Thy feet
I lay them down—a humble offering,
But all I have: The songs thou bad'st me sing,
  My love, my dreams of fame, my last heartbeat.
  Yea, I would make the sacrifice complete,
Nor for myself retain one precious thing.

Take Thou that narrow self, and let it be
  One with Thy vast Self; for the road is dark
  Whereby I travel, and my soul's lone spark
Yearns for the parent Flame. Or, make of me—
  If for that boon unfit—a warning mark
Upon the reefs of life's uncharted sea.

THE SONG OF MY SOUL

LONG did I wonder what my soul might be.
   Was it a pale reflection of God's light
Upon the surface of terrestrial night?
Was it the memory of eternity
Hidden behind the world-veil from my sight?
There came no answer, though I questioned long,
Until one day I heard my soul's own song:
"I am the spirit of Love that burns in thee
And in all things, quivering to reunite."

THE SINGER

IF any rumours of my humble days
　　Be blown along the dusty roads of time,
　May they not be of one who built the rhyme
But as a higher business; nor in praise
Of all-triumphant wrong disgraced the bays
　　Won by true singers in a worthier clime;
　　Nor on the mighty masters' paradigm
Broidered the ornaments of empty phrase.

But may those rumours be of one whose lyre
　　Was the deep voice of the imprisoned soul,
Whose mystic incantations could inspire
　　Visions, and power to read Life's hidden scroll:
Pain's purpose, and the meaning of desire—
　　The urge that drives us toward the unknown goal.

NOTE

THE FROZEN GRAIL, which Commander Peary carried with him to the North Pole, was originally published in the New York *Times*, on the day when he started for the Arctic. Other poems in this collection have appeared in *The Atlantic Monthly, The Century, The Forum, The Bookman, Lippincott's, The Smart Set, The Craftsman, Munsey's, The New Age, The Cosmopolitan, The Woman's Home Companion, The Metropolitan,* and *Everybody's*. Thanks are due to the editors of these magazines for the courteous permission to reprint.

RETURN TO the circulation desk of any
University of California Library
or to the

NORTHERN REGIONAL LIBRARY FACILITY
Bldg. 400, Richmond Field Station
University of California
Richmond, CA 94804-4698

ALL BOOKS MAY BE RECALLED AFTER 7 DAYS
2-month loans may be renewed by calling
 (415) 642-6233
1-year loans may be recharged by bringing books
 to NRLF
Renewals and recharges may be made 4 days
 prior to due date

DUE AS STAMPED BELOW

DUE NRLF APR 2 7 1989

Vuong, V.
3-24-89.
A 131
SENT ON ILL

JUL 30 2001

U. C. BERKELEY

Lightning Source UK Ltd.
Milton Keynes UK
UKHW011817050319
338540UK00022B/866/P